A Grandmother to Remember

BY DEANA BOGGESS

ISBN: 978-0-9994208-2-9
First Printing 2018
Editing by Diane Krause
Interior design by Lindsey Cousins
Artwork by Madison Wright
Cover design by Lindsey Cousins
Back cover photo by Cory Weaver
Southern Road Press
www.southernroadpress.com

For my grandchildren
Jack, Chloe, Tolkien, Jovita and any others that may follow.

May the imprints of your grandparents, from all generations, strengthen your faith.

Contents

Introduction

One of my favorite things to do is write. If I am sad I know my best therapy is to make a cup of coffee, sit in a quiet place, and write. When I am happy, I pack up my things and head to a coffee shop so I can people watch, and of course, write. I love the power of words, the comfort of words, and the legacy of words.

In the last few weeks, while I have had both sad and happy moments, I haven't been able to write. It may sound strange, but it feels like losing one of my best friends.

I took a break from writing to read one of my favorite books from childhood, *Little Women* by Louisa May Alcott. When I came to the part where Professor Bhaer tells Jo to write what she is passionate about and to tell the story only she can tell, I was inspired. I took off my glasses, turned to my husband and asked him what I was passionate about. What is the story that only I can tell? Without hesitation he said, "Being a grandmother!"

I *am* passionate about being a grandmother. I had no idea how much this role would mean to me and the joy it would bring to my life.

As for the story only I can tell, I am going to introduce you to a grandmother who left a beautiful imprint on my life. Of course, I have numerous cousins who could tell you all about her, but this is my story to tell—my own experiences and perceptions of Mary Bernice Moser Stone, known to us as Grandma

Stone. My cousins have their own story to tell, and my hope is that this book takes them back to their own memories and the lessons they learned.

This book is for my brothers and my cousins
David, Mark, Larry, Debbie, Tim, Becky, Elaine, TJ,
Brad, Tashia and Jessica
in honor of
Mary Bernice Moser Stone, also known as Grandma Stone,
in celebration of her 105th birthday.

A Letter to Grandmothers

As I prepared to write this book I realized how significantly the perception of a grandmother has evolved over just the past two generations. On one extreme, more grandparents than ever are raising grandchildren. According to pbs.org, 2.7 million grandparents are raising grandchildren in the United States, a seven percent increase from 2009.[1] On the other hand, I hear of many families where the grandparents are not engaged with their grandchildren. This may be due to distance since families are spread across the country but could also be influenced by the number of grandparents continuing careers into their sixties and seventies.

I suppose every generation of grandparents has been discouraged at times over changes in their culture and how it affects the youth. During my tenure as a grandparent, I have been extremely discouraged by the dangers of the internet, violent video games, and most distressing, school shootings. We all have opportunities to affect change, but as a grandparent we have a unique opportunity and position of influence. Just because our kids are grown does not mean our influence is over. We have our grandchildren to think of!

I have written this book in honor of my grandmother and in dedication to my grandchildren. I hope the stories I share will be meaningful to you and encourage you to be more intentional about the opportunities of influence you have as a grandparent.

I encourage you to gather a group of grandmothers together to talk about your relationships with your own grandparents, the imprints they left on your lives, and brainstorm together on how you can leave the most life-changing imprint on your grandchildren. At the end of each chapter, I've included a section titled Questions for the Grandmother to prompt those discussions.

Following the discussion questions is a Making Memories section with lots of ideas for interacting with your grandchildren. I hope you will take some of my suggestions and go on an adventure with them.

Maybe you know someone who will soon be a grandmother and you can encourage them with this book so they, too, can leave an intentional imprint on their grandchildren. (It would make a great baby shower gift for the grandmother-to-be!)

Your experience, wisdom, faith, and love are the best gifts you can give your grandchildren. You have a story no one else can tell. May you share it with intention, purpose, faith and love.

Blessings,
Deana

Bedtime Stories

The three-paneled door creaked as Grandma opened it. The house quieted as everyone prepared for bed. There had just been a family gathering or celebration and there were people all over the house settling in for the night. My three closest cousins—in age and gender—and I were lined up on the pull-out sofa in Grandma and Grandpa's room. If any of us turned over in the night, the rest of us would know it but we didn't mind because we loved being together and felt we had the place of honor. After all, we were in Grandma and Grandpa's room.

As we settled into our bed of old family quilts and slept in one of the original hide-a-beds with squeaky springs and lumps in the mattress, we waited for Grandma to finish changing. I always found it interesting that Grandma would change just behind the door and you could see the garments as they passed by the crack in the door. Grandma was always very modest and always expected her daughters and granddaughters to be modest as well, yet only an open door was between us. It is a memory that doesn't really matter in the whole scheme of things but when you are a kid, you think about such things.

I remember sweet, gentle Grandpa often saying, "We need to get these kids to bed," mostly because he was ready for bed! And Grandma, well she would keep the night going by asking, "Who wants to tell the bedtime story?"

Becky, Elaine, Tammy and I would poke each other, trying to get the other cousin to tell the story but inevitably it would be Grandma who would share the story for the night. I don't recall specifics of the stories she would tell but I do recall how they made me feel. They made me feel loved, valued and safe. We all knew Grandma and Grandpa loved us and would always be there for us. I never thought of Grandma and Grandpa as rich, yet they provided everything we needed — love, security, memories, sodas in the refrigerator, and a good bedtime story to drift off to.

Much of my identity as a grandmother has been focused around stories as well. I have loved picking up my grandson, Jack, from school. On those occasions, we would usually have forty-five minutes together and one of my favorite expressions from Jack has been, "Meme, tell me another story from when you were a kid." Oftentimes, I would slip in an exaggeration to see if he would catch it and he usually did. As a young reader, he enjoyed diaries and stories with stick figures and cartoons in them and I loved to label the figures with people's names from the family or add balloon sayings to make things a little more interesting. I treasure Jack's mind as he has taken on learning both English and Spanish. He loves helping me with a Spanish accent and rolling my R's, and I love challenging him with math facts and problems just as my uncle did for me when I was a kid.

My oldest granddaughter, Chloe, is a lover of books. She dreams of going to unusual bookstores and finding a treasure to bring home with her. Just as I would find my oldest daughter reading in the bathtub in the middle of the night, you can also find Chloe sneaking up after the lights are off to read just one more chapter. Over the years we have had Bible studies, book clubs and book exchanges. Chloe feels my literary experience has been limited because I haven't spent enough time with books of fantasy and I love to coax her into the classics, the books without the flashy pictures but the comfort of the past. I suppose we are literary accountability partners of sorts.

I recently bought each of the kids a book and filled the books with surprises, such as a picture of their mothers when they were little, pretty postcards, sticky notes telling them how much I love them, and even a dollar or two. They had to promise me they wouldn't skip ahead to claim all the prizes but let them be their reward as they stumble upon them.

My youngest grandson, Tolkien, and I are bonding over board books and picture books of animals. With a two-year-old, every picture is a new adventure full of new words and experiences. You just can't cultivate a love for stories too early. Even my sweet little Jovita—Jack's baby sister—will be reading books with me in no time, some in English and some in Spanish.

Questions for the Grandmother

- Do you have memories of listening to stories your grandmother told?
- Do you remember being curled up in your grandmother's lap and listening to her read?
- What stories will you most want your grandchildren to hear?
- What books will you be sure to add to your grandchildren's library?
- What surprises can you add to your story time to make it more memorable?

Making Memories with Storytime

- Read your favorite childhood story.
- Find one of your childhood books and read it to your grandchildren.
- Write a story for your grandchildren and self-publish it.
- Write a story with your grandchildren and self-publish it.
- Read aloud a chapter book and then go see the movie or play of the book.
- Go to an unusual spot to have story time together.
- Invite a storyteller over to your house and make a special snack for your grandchildren.
- Put on a play with your grandchildren.
- Find one of your children's special books and give it to your grandchildren.
- Create a special spot in your house for bedtime stories.
- Decorate a guest bedroom in the theme of your grandchild's favorite book.
- Have your grandchildren join you in bed for the bedtime story. Be sure to let Grandpa read to them too.
- Hide little gifts inside the bedtime book for them to find. Have the gifts correlate with the story.
- Go outside and read under the stars.
- Set up a tent in the living room, turn off the lights, and read a story with a flashlight.
- Be sure to add variety to your reading materials such as chapter books, picture books, pop-up books, short stories, tall tales, magazines, comics, and poetry.

Flowers

What a beautiful day it was to go on a walk. Tolkien and I love to go on walks together and explore. Tolkien loves to talk about "sits" (chairs and sofas). He asks me to make sits for him out of all kinds of things and tries to sit on them no matter what their size. He was so excited when we went for a walk in a big store full of all kinds of sits!

This particular day was different. We were going on a walk outside to explore the historic streets of downtown Round Rock. My favorite store wasn't open yet, so we went up and down the sidewalk, window shopping and watching the waterfall in the water park. We gradually made our way to my favorite store and walked in to find a little treasure for the day. Tolkien was fascinated by the "moo-moos" and "neigh-neighs" he saw on the walls and I was interested in a new candle. We all have our preferences on scents. I don't like candles that smell too sweet and definitely don't like candles that smell like food (I have enough food issues, thank you!). After smelling twenty different candles, the saleslady suggested a new scent, "Just Picked Flowers." She said, "You will feel like you just walked into a flower shop!"

Well, that comment caught my attention. Grandma always worked in a flower shop and managed Bruce Flowers in Wichita Falls, Texas for years. I hesitated to open the candle and told the lady, "I don't know if this will make me happy or sad" and then I told her about Grandma Stone.

I opened the candle and was flooded with memories of Grandma Stone and flowers—lots of flowers. The aroma did not make me sad, it just made me grateful. Grateful for her love, her presence in my life, and her desire to teach me new things. As you can imagine, I couldn't leave the store without bringing Grandma home with me.

I suppose I love freeform flower arrangements more than professionally designed ones. I love a beautiful backyard garden that supplies flowers for the kitchen table, free of charge. I love the wildflowers and weeds picked by grandchildren proud to bring their Meme a nice bouquet. The petals may be falling off and the stems may be squished but that little bouquet is full of love. Nevertheless, my love of flowers came from Grandma Stone.

A tradition I started years ago with my daughters was to read the book, *Mandy* by Julie Andrews. I have always loved Julie Andrews and when I stumbled on her children's book, I fell in love with it. My daughters and I read it many summers and were inspired by Mandy's transformation of a little cottage overrun by weeds and tall grasses that she turned into every little girl's dream garden. As I plant flowers in the backyard I think about my grandchildren and how I hope they will feel like they are in Mandy's garden ready to create and explore.

Questions for the Grandmother

- What scents remind you of your grandmother?
- Are you afraid to encounter scents from the past? Or do you embrace them with gratitude?
- What scents do you want your grandchildren to remember?
- What scents will they associate with you? Flowers, fresh-baked bread, cookies fresh out of the oven, or fresh copies of lecture notes from your latest presentation?

Making Memories with Flowers

- Learn how to make flowers out of tissue paper and make a large bouquet.
- Learn and memorize the wildflowers that grow in your area.
- Take your grandchildren, two easels, paints, and a camera to a field of flowers and paint.
- Learn about edible flowers and make a flowering feast together.
- Make a beautiful bouquet of flowers out of handprints and thumbprints.
- Go to your local grocery store, buy some flowers and Mason jars. Make bouquets and deliver them to people that might need some cheering up.
- Read about May Day and deliver some surprise bouquets.
- Plant a garden of beautiful flowers in the yard. Let this be their own special spot.
- Build a fairy garden in the backyard. Just be sure to include the flowers!
- Go on a field trip to a botanical garden, unusual nursery, or a wildflower center.

Work

When I was a little girl I would often go to Grandma and Grandpa's house to spend the week. I loved spending time with them and especially enjoyed going to work at the flower shop with Grandma. We would get up very early in the morning before the sun was even up. I remember bouncing around on the floor of the flower truck. (This was before being required to ride in a seat with a seatbelt.) Sometimes we had deliveries to make, sometimes we stopped for a breakfast snack, but we were always up early. My brothers and I still refer to an early morning as a "Grandma Stone morning."

When we arrived at the flower shop I was always greeted by Grandma's employees and a dear great-aunt who also worked there. I was given a seat of honor on a tall stool and for a while, I sat on top of a phone book as well. I was placed before the work table and was given a job to do such as wrapping wires, cutting foam or handing flowers to Grandma to be arranged. After watching all the ladies design bouquets, I would get down and walk around the flower shop to see the different arrangements. I especially loved the china figurines of little girls interspersed among the flowers.

The treat for the day was to walk down to the drug store and buy a soda or root beer float at the old-fashioned soda fountain. I remember the floor of that soda fountain, because there were coins glued to the floor and my brothers and

I would try to pick up the money.

A few years ago my husband participated in the "Hotter'N Hell" bike race in Wichita Falls. While he was sweating in the 100-degree heat I asked my GPS to take me to Bruce Flowers. After forty years had passed most of the landmarks had changed but I finally found the store by the address and went inside. I told the store owner who I was and about my quest, but she had no connection to my grandparents as there had been many owners since my grandmother was there. She said I might remember one thing though and led me to the back of the store. There on the floor was the original tile. I was disappointed that so much had changed but grateful for at least one memory preserved.

In some respects, Grandma was ahead of her time managing a flower shop. She taught me the value of hard work, how to be joyful with your employees, and kind to your customers.

Fortunately, I was able to bring my grandchildren to work with me during the years I taught a bridge-to-kindergarten class. My granddaughter attended the preschool and when she was old enough, I had the pleasure of having her as one of my students. I loved sharing my love for literature and learning with her. At the end of the day she would sit on the top of my desk and we would have a little snack together.

My grandson would come visit the classroom as much as possible. If he had a day off from his regular school, he would come with me and join in on the class. All of my students knew who he was and one of them suggested I make a nameplate for him so he had his own place when he came to visit. Chloe, Jack and I spent many summers having "Meme Camp" learning how to read and exploring all kinds of topics.

I dream of someday taking my grandchildren with me to speak, sell books and train teachers. Someday...

I have retired from teaching now and my youngest grandchildren will never be in my classroom, but I will take every opportunity I can to show them what it means to work hard, to love your co-workers, and love your work. My message will be the same, it will just be in a different place.

Questions for the Grandmother

- Did your grandmother work outside the home? If so, what was her occupation?
- What skills did your grandmother teach you?
- What did she teach you about work ethic?
- What are the work principles you desire to pass on?
- What skills will you teach your grandchildren?
- Will they remember you as a grandmother who rose early in the morning or stayed up with them late at night?

Making Memories with Work

- Tell your grandchildren about your very first job, what your responsibilities were, and how much you were paid.
- Over time, tell your grandchildren about each of your jobs, what your responsibilities were, how much you were paid, and the lessons you learned from the job.
- Explore what your grandchildren would like to do when they grow up. Take them to visit someone who currently does that job.
- Give your grandchildren chores around the house and pay them for the work they do.
- Discuss taking an overnight trip with your grandchildren and plan out how much it will cost. Discuss ways you can all work to earn the money to go. Work on this together and make sure it will take at least a couple of weeks to earn enough money. The harder they work, the bigger the reward!
- If you or Grandpa are still working, take them to visit your place of work. Introduce them to people and let them see what you do. When you get paid, take your grandchildren along and cash the check. No matter what you make, they will think it is a lot of money. Then "pay" bills with the money so they can understand that much of your paycheck is already designated to pay a bill. This will help them understand the value of money.
- Have either you or their parents pay them a weekly allowance. Set up three jars—one for saving, one for tithing, and one for spending.

Family Gatherings

When I was a little girl, it only took two and a half hours to get from our house in Dallas to Grandma and Grandpa Stone's house in Wichita Falls, Texas but for much of my life it was a fourteen-hour drive from our home in Denver, Colorado to Texas. For summer visits it meant surviving the Texas heat and the sounds of cicadas. In the winter it meant driving through the snow and getting over mountain passes. My brothers and I would fight over seats in the old paneled station wagon, often fighting over who would be fortunate enough to fall asleep in the wheel wells as Dad drove. I remember exclaiming with excitement when my brothers were sound asleep, "There is Wichita Falls!" loud enough to wake them up but then realize that Grandma's house was still hours away.

Our excitement would grow as we saw the lights of the city approaching, knowing we were almost "home." As we pulled into the driveway of their house, the distinctive sound of tires going over gravel told us we were home. Grandma and Grandpa would be at the screen door to greet us. We would give them hugs and ask when the rest of the family would be arriving, and we would anxiously wait.

The excitement grew as each family arrived. "My, how you have grown" was expressed by every aunt and uncle and it just wasn't right until I heard my Aunt Joyce say, "You have freckles on you but you're pretty." It was her way of saying, "I love you."

After everyone arrived and we had caught up on stories and happenings, we would turn into bed. There were people in the guest room, people on the living room sofa, pallets on the dining room floor, people on the family room sofa, people in the back bedroom and of course, Grandma and Grandpa and the girls in their room. We could have as many as twenty-four people in that 2,000-square-foot house but we were happy — extremely happy!

In the morning we would hear Grandma busy in the kitchen and we would pull the covers over our heads in hopes of getting a little more sleep. After a few minutes, however, we realized there was a lot of fun to be had and we would jump out of bed. It was important to be quick because twenty-four people and one bathroom means you want to be first in line! There was another bathroom in the back room, but the door had a skeleton key and all the grandkids were afraid of it.

Grandma and the women of the family would start working on breakfast as the grandchildren ran outside to play. In no time at all the smells of bacon and eggs, oats, and homemade cinnamon rolls would call us in. As quick as we ran in, we ran back out to rake the leaves in the yard and jump in the piles or play games in the backyard. I remember playing volleyball and my cousin Becky, in a heavy southern drawl, yelling at me, "Rear up and hit it, Deana. Rear up and hit it!"

Later in the day we would play Jacks on the back porch, dress dolls with the clothes our great-great aunt had made or play a lively game of Spoons. Before we knew it, it would be time to eat again. It didn't occur to me until many years later that the women must have gone from making one meal to cleaning it up and within minutes start preparing for the next one. I don't remember the women complaining because they were catching up on their jobs and the news in their families. The men were all in the living room playing dominoes for hours upon hours.

Later in the day my great-grandparents would join us. They were the keepers of history and tradition and I savored every hint of it. Several tables were put together to stretch across the living and dining rooms so we would each have a place to sit. As we gathered, Grandpa Moser would lead the dinner prayer, which reminded me of an Indian chant. I later learned that he did not know how to read or write and was afraid of making a mistake, so he would memorize and recite his prayers. It makes me sad that one of us grandchildren would start to snicker as he prayed and then the rest of us would follow. As children, we had no idea how much wisdom was behind those prayers.

After dinner we were tired and always wondered what to do. Inevitably we ended up gathered around Grandma's cedar chest full of pictures. We would make fun of each other's school pictures sometimes, but we always loved talking about the memories that came to mind as we pulled each picture out of the chest. Sometimes I wondered why Grandma didn't put the pictures in albums but maybe she knew how much fun we had pulling them out of the cedar chest.

I guess I always thought our children and grandchildren would have the same experience until I suddenly realized it would be different. But I also came to realize that although they would not have the same memories I had as a child, they would have memories special to them.

I love when the grandchildren come over to our house. I have a picture wall of their ancestors, a picture wall of their mommas growing up, and of course a wall of their pictures as they grow up. My hope is to convey the message that family matters and they are an important part of the family.

I also want them to have a sense of curiosity when they come over, so I leave boxes of polished rocks and bowls of seashells for them to look through. There is also a treehouse and flower gardens to play in, forts to be built in the living room and stories to be read in the library. We may not be wealthy, but we have plenty and we love to have them sit on our laps and enjoy what we have.

Questions for the Grandmother

- Did you visit your grandparents when you were a child?
- What were your relationships like?
- Did you gather with cousins?
- What did you enjoy exploring at your grandparents' house?
- What games did you play?
- Do you make it a special event when your grandchildren walk through your door even if you saw them yesterday?
- What games do you play with them?
- Have you introduced them to the games you played as a child?
- Have you shared pictures of ancestors with your grandchildren?
- Do you have things in your home that cultivate curiosity, creativity, and exploration?

Making Memories with Family Gatherings

- Have the family over for an old-fashioned pie-throwing contest.
- Have a whipped cream fight in the backyard.
- Set up a table outside and let the children play with shaving cream.
- Set up a mud pit in the backyard. I guarantee you they will have fun. Just be sure to have a water hose ready!
- Let the grandchildren plan and prepare dinner for the rest of the family.
- Have the grandchildren put on plays or share new dance moves with the rest of the family.
- Have the grandchildren come over and help with a big project such as painting, building, gardening, working on a car. There is no better way for them to learn than by watching you!
- Have the grandchildren over to learn the basics of caring for a car: changing a tire, changing the oil, checking fluids and washing a car.
- Pop some popcorn and have the family over to watch family videos.
- Have the family over to sit by the cedar chest of pictures and go through them.
- Have lemonade stands, garage sales, and craft shows to help the grandchildren earn money. Then take them shopping!
- Make some homemade ice cream or snow ice cream together. They will love it and remember it well!

Food

––––––––––––   ❀   ––––––––––––

Grandma Stone often made a connection with loved ones through food. Whenever there was a family gathering Grandma always had a crystal dish sitting on the glass shelf next to the kitchen. It was low enough for everyone to be able to reach it and was filled with chocolate stars. I rarely remember eating one because I knew those were really for my Uncle Steve.

My special food was fried okra. I loved fried okra! Not only did Grandma make sure she always prepared it for me, but she would often serve me first. She didn't want the okra to make it around that big long table and be all gone before it had reached my plate. The last time I went to see Grandma my brother and I drove with my two daughters (Bethany was three and Sarah was an infant) to Texas to say goodbye. Grandma had colon cancer and was in her last few months of life. I will never forget seeing my grandmother on the sofa cutting the okra in a bowl to make sure I would have some for dinner.

Grandma made other special efforts. I know she made homemade cinnamon rolls for my older two brothers and plenty of homemade rolls for my little brother. Maybe there wasn't a special food prepared for everyone in the family, but Grandma found all kinds of ways to make sure every family member felt valued and loved.

It makes me laugh now to see how much food customs have changed. When

I grew up, most of our food was cooked in bacon grease. We had all kinds of carbs, fat, sugar, and butter! I suppose it was kept in balance by all the fresh vegetables brought in from Great-Grandpa Moser's farm.

Another significant difference in food from then to now was leaving the food out all day. The leftovers from breakfast were left on the table with a tablecloth over them and the leftovers from lunch were covered until dinner. Don't get me wrong—I'm not recommending this practice. I am just saying it was common in those days, and we never got sick.

Today, when our immediate family gathers, there are ten people around the table. When my mother and brothers and their families join us, there can be as many as nineteen, two of which join us in our hearts from heaven. I can't say I have everyone's favorite food at every meal, but I do the best I can to make the rounds. I do try to make sure there are plenty of black olives so the grandkids can put one on each of their fingers to eat. The adults better grab one quick before they are all gone!

Food isn't left out all day, but I do wait to wash all the dishes because I would much rather spend my time visiting than washing. Pa will go in the kitchen and start, and I always plead with him to wait and come join the conversation, but his love language is acts of service and mine is time spent with loved ones so that is usually how it ends up!

After dinner the older grandchildren usually put on a show for the adults. We have been known to exit the building, come back in with tickets, and patiently wait for the show to begin. What I love the most is that the children don't feel any inhibition and they dance or sing their little hearts out. They know we love them and will cheer them on no matter what. I dread the day the kids stop dancing but luckily for us, the second wave of grandchildren will take over where they left off!

Questions for the Grandmother

- What special foods do you remember eating when you visited your grandparents?
- Do you know what each of your children and grandchildren love to eat the most?
- How do you like to spoil your grandchildren?
- Are there special habits or traditions that occur around food in your family?
- Do you have a family prayer before the meal? Who leads it?
- What is your love language when it comes to your family?

Making Memories with Food

- Get out your first cookbook and make something together from it.
- Buy your grandchildren cookbooks they picked out.
- On Grandchildren's Day have your grandchildren over for dinner and make each of their favorites (it is totally okay if the dishes don't really go together).
- Compile a book of family recipes from several generations.
- Have an extra refrigerator in the garage filled with water and a variety of drinks. It will save wear and tear on the screen door and will allow more time for fun!
- With their parents' permission, let the kids go to bed but tell them there will be a special time with grandma and grandpa after the parents go to bed. Then go in with flashlights, gather the children, and pile into a tent in the backyard for a little story time and snacks.
- Have a special placemat made for each grandchild. It can have a special picture of something that interests them and of course, put their name on it. You can make these and laminate them at a teacher's store or let them make them one afternoon! Of course, you'll want to serve some great snacks on their new placemats!
- Serve a multi-course meal, with the courses in reverse order. It won't hurt them to start with dessert!

- Have the children create a cookbook. They can dictate how to make one of their favorite recipes and you can type them up and have them copied and assembled. They can even draw pictures to accompany the recipes. It will make a great Christmas present for the rest of the family.
- Find an unusual place to have a picnic—on top of a table, in the master bath, on the driveway, in the car with the windows rolled down, in a treehouse, or on grandma and grandpa's bed.
- Take the kids to the grocery store and let one of them pick out an appetizer, one pick out an entree, one pick out a side, and one pick out a dessert. It could be interesting!
- Spend an evening having a progressive dinner. Go to one restaurant for an appetizer, another restaurant for the main course, and another restaurant for dessert

Quilts

It wasn't long after our visit with Grandma Stone that she passed from this life into heaven. I was so grateful I had the opportunity to go back and visit her one last time and introduce her to her newest great-grandchild, my daughter Sarah.

I had experienced the passing of two great-grandparents but Grandma Stone was the first grandparent I had said goodbye to. I had an emptiness in my heart that I had never experienced before and the realization that we all will die someday was now a reality I wasn't sure I was ready for.

I let myself walk through the loneliness and pain of losing Grandma for several months and then I started to look for something to bring me comfort. Just as the warm quilts on the sofa bed my cousins and I shared had brought comfort to me, the ones she had made for my home gave me solace as well. I appreciated the quilt she made for our wedding and the one she made for my birthday a couple of years before her passing. I had never noticed all the stitches before and the skill and patience she had to keep the stitches all the same length. The gift of quilts had become a treasure.

It wasn't long before I needed a new level of comfort. The best way I could think of to stay close to Grandma was to start quilting myself. I had to stretch my brain a little to be able to make the intricate designs but quilting soon became a time of prayer and meditation. I made about twenty-five quilts and that was a special time in my life. Although I have set aside the skill for now, I am thankful for the years it helped me get through.

I have eight of Grandma's quilts in my home. They have comforted my children and grandchildren, nursed a grandchild through scarlet fever, and helped make many forts and pallets in the living room. The quilt I treasure the most is the handkerchief quilt my dad had. Mom kindly passed it on to me after my father passed and she moved into a smaller place. The handkerchiefs came from a variety of women in the family.

Sometimes Grandma's quilts were simply made of scraps and sometimes they were artistically planned for an individual, but always, they were made of love.

Questions for the Grandmother

- Do you remember any quilts in your grandmother's home? Describe one of them.
- Do you have any special memories about quilts as you were growing up?
- Is there a quilt in the family you would like to have? Is there a special story behind it?
- Do you have a quilt you plan to pass down to one of your grandchildren?
- Have you ever considered making a quilt for each grandchild? If so, who would it be for and what would it look like?

Making Memories with Quilts

- Have your grandchildren over to learn about quilts and how they were used to preserve history and even provide a map to help people flee from slavery.
- Take your grandchildren to a quilt show and have them show you which ones are their favorites.
- Have your grandchildren design a quilt out of construction paper.
- Assist your grandchildren in making a simple Amish quilt.
- Make a lap size quilt with blocks that can be written in. Write all the cute things your grand-children say in each of the blocks. Be sure to research the best type of pen to use.
- Applique your grandchild's favorite fictional characters on a quilt. I made one for my daughter with a design of all her favorite characters having a tea party together. I even included her "lovey!"
- Make a t-shirt quilt for your grandchild's graduation. You can pay someone to quilt it on a machine pretty reasonably.
- Take your grandchildren to a quilt shop to pick out fabrics and either make a quilt together or give it to them on a special occasion.
- Make a great fort or teepee out of a fun quilt.
- Have a special tea party with quilts as the decor.
- Make a quilt out of fabrics from clothes your grandchildren have outgrown. This will take some planning, but for example, a quilt made from girls' Easter or Christmas dresses would be fun.

Faith

Bedtime stories, flowers, work, family gatherings, food, and quilts all possess their own class of memories of Grandma Stone but what I most value and appreciate are the memories and expressions of faith.

I remember attending church with Grandma as a little girl. On Sunday mornings she always put on her best dress, prayed, studied her Bible, and had dinner planned and often ready before we even left the house. While Grandma was getting ready, my grandfather was on his way to the farm to pick up my great-grandfather.

When we arrived at the church she would get great-grandpa settled and everyone would make sure to greet her. Grandma was well known and respected at her church. She had a place of honor and I was honored simply because I was her granddaughter. She often told people I was the granddaughter who looked like her. I couldn't imagine why they thought I had gray hair, age spots, and wrinkles, but I did hope people could see joy and a deep faith in my face, just like Grandma's. She was one of the most beautiful women in the world to me.

My grandparents were Methodists so Methodist traditions and liturgy are the ones woven in my faith from childhood. I remember attending Sunday school and often being called on for answers to questions. Sunday school teachers often assumed I would know the answer to their questions since I was Bernice's granddaughter and my father was a Methodist minister. I was always sad, and often ashamed, if I didn't know the answer. I'm not complaining about them—I put the pressure on myself. I wished I knew as much as they did about the Bible.

One memory of Grandma is deeply implanted in my heart. I would often hear her up early in the morning and I would hear the loud rattling sound of a pressure cooker on the stove. To be honest the sound annoyed me, and I wondered why Grandma had to do it so early in the morning, but I had no idea what she was really doing.

If I hadn't heard that rattling sound I never would have known she was up. Many years later I learned that she was up praying for everyone in the family. She prayed for each of us by name and knowing Grandma, she was praying about the struggles she knew each of us had but she never mentioned. There were so many of us it would take some time to pray for each one of us. We don't all walk the path of faith Grandma did, but you have to respect the love, commitment, and the sacrifice Grandma made for each of us. She loved us, and more than anything wanted us to experience the love of God as she did.

Today the old hymns sung in church are being replaced by contemporary music. Traditions and customs are being replaced by new ones and the church pews are being replaced by stadium seating. In my house I keep an old church pew that God brought me, with a sign hanging over it on which are the words "How Great Thou Art." They remind me of the faith of my great-grandparents, my grandparents, and my parents. They remind me of the faith in which I was raised.

One of my greatest regrets is that I didn't ask Grandma more questions about her faith. Many times over the years I have fantasized about visiting Grandma in heaven and asking her all kinds of questions about faith and God. It is because of those regrets that I do everything I can to pass my faith on to my own grandchildren. Most likely my grandchildren don't realize that our time together will be short. They don't know that I won't always be here so that is why I write books like these. My life will not last forever but hopefully my words will and when they come to that time in their lives when they are reflecting on my faith and what I might do in their circumstances, hopefully my words will minister to them in some way. Written words last for generations.

So, my dear sweet grandchildren, let me leave a gift to you…

Please know that I loved the Lord with all my heart. I committed my life to Jesus Christ when I was thirteen. I told Him He was my Lord and my Savior and I wanted to follow Him. When I was in college I started to question my faith because I needed to make it my own and not my parents'. I pleaded with God to spare my life until I had it all worked out in my mind. Soon after, he spared me in a car accident driving home from college.

As an adult I struggled with the balance between legalism and grace and through the help of a pastor, landed on grace. For so many years I struggled to be the "perfect Christian" until I accepted that I never could be. So now

I try to take each day at a time being grateful for the grace He extends to me whenever I fall short and for the joy I feel walking in His path now and assured of His physical presence in the future. Life is crazy. Life is hard. We were never promised it would be easy but one thing I know for sure, I would never want to live this life without Him right by my side. God is good. He is faithful and walks every day of life right by our sides.

I have prayed many years of prayers over you, Jack, Chloe, Tolkien and Jovita. I loved praying for you in the morning, throughout the day and at night, that God would keep you safe, that you would know how deeply you are loved and that you would commit your life to Him and walk with Him. My prayers are out of love for you.

Remember those who led you,

who spoke the word of God to you;

and considering the result of their conduct,

imitate their faith.

Hebrews 13:7 (NASB)

Questions for the Grandmother

- Did you grow up with *faith genes*?
- What did you learn from your grandmother about faith?
- Do you wish you had asked more questions?
- Do you have a faith to pass on to your grandchildren?
- What do you most want them to know?
- Can they see your faith being lived out in your life?
- What do you think they will say about you when you pass?
- Have you made a commitment to pray for your grandchildren on a daily basis?
- What are some ways you can invest in their spiritual development?

Making Memories Through Sharing Your Faith

- Share about your religious experience as a child. What did it mean to you?
- Write your personal testimony out for your grandchildren to read now or in the future.
- If possible, take your grandchildren to see the church you grew up in.
- Consider getting baptized with your grandchildren and have a celebration afterward.
- Read Bible stories together.
- Have a weekly Bible study together.
- Share about the spiritual heritage of their grandparents, great-grandparents, and great-great-grandparents.
- Make a video sharing your faith with your grandchildren.
- Write spiritual stories for children and self-publish them for your grandchildren.
- When your grandchildren are older take them to a church that is different than their experience such as an Indian reservation or a cowboy church. Talk about the similarities and the differences between their church experience and the one they just attended.
- Pay for your grandchildren to go on a retreat or mission trip.
- Participate in a mission trip with your grandchildren.
- Sponsor a child through an organization and write letters together. You and your grandchildren pray for the child on a regular basis.
- Encourage your grandchildren to keep a diary of their spiritual growth.

- You keep a diary of your grandchildren's spiritual growth from your perspective and share it with them many years from now.
- Take a hike up to a summit, have a picnic, and talk about God's beautiful creation.
- Visit a farm and discuss some of the farm parables in the Bible. Here are a few to get you started:
  Matthew 13:3-9, 18-23, Mark 4:3-9, 14-20, Luke 8:4-8, Luke 8:11-15, Matthew 21:33-41, Mark 12:1-11, Luke 20:9-18
- Take them to lunch with someone you look up to spiritually and tell them why you look up to that person.
- Look up the meaning of your grandchild's name and pray it over them. Share why their parents gave them that name.
- Share the meaning of your name and ask them if it fits you.
- Take your grandchildren shopping for a Bible. Guide them on their choices so it is appropriate but give them as much freedom as you can.
- Create a painting that symbolizes your faith and have them make one as well.
- Buy a plaster kit and make a cast of you and your grandchild holding hands together. Be sure to put the date on the bottom, as well as your ages.

Generational Lessons

I had the opportunity to teach Grandma about the power and pain of words. As a child of the early 1900s and an adult of the 1930s, Grandma sometimes used words that were commonplace to her, but soul-piercing to others. Just as she taught me, I hope I taught her. Her childhood lessons were from The Great Depression and World War II and mine were from the dawn of the Civil Rights Movement. Our children lived through the bombing of the World Trade Center and the realization that as nations, we are all vulnerable. Our grandchildren are living through the questions of #metoo, gender equality, gender identity, racism, and immigration. There are many more issues, causes and questions to each of these eras, but my simplification illustrates the changing of the times.

I remember seeing the angst on Grandma's face as she watched the times change. She would often ask me questions about it, but I never felt judgment. One thing I knew for certain—she was always praying about it.

Now as a grandmother of four, I understand that angst. I am deeply troubled over the changes occurring and often feel helpless to change it. It kind of makes me smile to think that someday my children will understand those feelings, as the truths and perceptions they grew up with are challenged and their children's generation starts to think differently.

I suppose what helps me the most is to think about the grace I have been granted and extend the same grace to others. I am sure my dyed jet-black hair and army fatigues upset my mother, but she just loved and accepted me through it. (I definitely loved and accepted my children but I probably voiced my opinion way too often. Sorry, kids!)

As with all people, we need to get to know their story. The best way to close the generation gap is to hear kids' stories. See them as people trying to figure out life just as we did. They need time spent with them. They need love. They need acceptance. And well, they probably need to hear *your* story so they can understand you better. This section is brief, but I hope you will spend some time looking through the suggestions and try a few. Experiences around generational lessons will teach you more than anything I can say!

Questions for the Grandmother

- What changes did your grandmother struggle with?
- What changes did your mother struggle with?
- How did their struggles make you feel?
- As a grandmother, what cultural changes scare you or make you feel uncomfortable?
- What teenage personality type is the hardest for you to understand? Have you made efforts to try to understand?

Making Memories with Generational Lessons

- Learn a dance move from one of your grandchildren.
- Teach them a dance move you knew as a kid.
- Have a dance party with your grandchildren.
- Go to your grandchild's favorite restaurant for dinner.
- Go see a movie with your grandchildren that they picked out.
- Have your grandchildren teach you all the slang words used today.
- Learn something new on the computer from your grandchildren.
- Prepare and share one of your favorite snacks such as a root beer float.
- Talk about current events with your grandchildren and be sure to listen and not judge.
- Go on a bike ride with your grandchildren.
- Learn the abbreviations (LOL, TTYL, BRB) of the day and use them during dinner conversation with your grandchildren.
- Share about a significant event in history from when you were a child. Share what you were doing at the time and how it made you feel.
- Talk about the drills that are done in school. Today schools have active shooter drills. You may have had tornado or bomb drills. Talk about fear and how to overcome it.
- Talk to your grandchildren about marriage. Share your wedding with them in whatever form you can. Be realistic about the challenges of marriage but also the blessings.

Love

One of the sorrows of my heart is when I scolded my grandson Jack for something he didn't do. I apologized profusely and he looked up at me with such innocent, forgiving eyes and said, "That's ok. We all make mistakes." What grace, what compassion, what love!

I still haven't forgiven myself for my mistake but I am so grateful he has. The love and bond between a grandparent and a grandchild is like no other. I truly loved being a parent. I read and studied for years about parenting, long before I became one. I prayed for my children every day. I sacrificed in every way I could. The reality was, however, I had to stay focused on a goal. I had to instill values and discipline and responsibility.

We have to do these things as grandparents as well but the freedoms that come along with it are such a blessing. I remember sacrificing for Jack as well. One day he had a presentation at his school and I wanted to attend. I was also caring for my youngest grandson that day, so I drove an hour east, then an hour south, then an hour north and then a half hour east to see his twenty-minute presentation. Did I mind? Not at all, because I loved my sweet Jack so much. Was I exhausted? Absolutely! As a grandparent I could come home and take as long a nap as I wanted. I could sleep the whole next day if I wanted but as a parent, you do not have that luxury. Jack will probably never know the sacrifice required that day, but my hope is that it adds to the pile of sacrifices that demonstrate how deep my love for him is. I would do it all again just so he would know how much I love him (and I would also come back home and take a nap!).

There are many memories our oldest grandchildren do not remember, and in a way, it makes me sad. I also know those situations have helped lay a foundation. A foundation that their parents are also building.

Train up a child in the way he should go, and even when he is old he will not depart from it. Proverbs 22:6

Through parenting, teaching, grandparenting and friendships, I have watched many children question and walk away from the foundation laid for them, but I have also watched them return. It may take thirty years or a couple of months to return, but the foundation stands. I once had a colonel share his perspective on parenting with me, which was: "Be consistent, persistent and pray." That advice has served me well and I have shared it many, many times.

My cousins and I may have traveled far on our journeys and we have all taken different paths at times but the foundation of love, acceptance and faith from Grandma Stone remained true. The foundation she laid never left us. She passed away twenty-eight years ago but her foundation of love remains under our feet and in our hearts.

Questions for the Grandmother

- What are the sacrifices you remember your grandparents making for you?
- What type of foundation did your grandmother lay for you?
- What do you want to pass on to your grandchildren? What changes do you want to make?
- What mistakes have you made with your grandchildren? Have you asked for forgiveness? Have you forgiven yourself?
- What do you want the foundation you lay to look like?
- What truths do you want to instill?
- How will you go about building a foundation of love and faith?
- How can you best partner with their parents?

Making Memories with Love

- I remember when I was five and my grandmother showed me a card that would be given to me on my sixteenth birthday. I thought it was the most beautiful card I had ever seen. I thought it was an eternity until I would be that old! Every couple of years I asked my grandmother if I could look at it for a minute. Is there something really special that you could tell your grandchild, "It will be yours someday…"?
- One day my grandchildren climbed out the bedroom window to play "Spy." I was very concerned about their safety. I did tell the parents because I wanted them to be aware of it for safety reasons, but I asked permission for it to stay between the grandchildren and me. Could I talk about it with them and let it stay between us? Our children were gracious to let me do that. Sometimes what happens at Meme's can stay at Meme's and that is ok.
- One of my favorite things in my house is the Love Chair in my library. It is a comfortable plain white chair and my grandchildren have drawn pictures and written notes to me over the years on it. I treasure it. Yes, at Meme and Pa's you can even draw on the furniture. Well, only one piece of furniture!
- When Chloe was just four years old and was learning how to write, Pa accidentally ran his hand through a table saw. Four surgeries totaling twenty-one hours were required to repair his hand. There were casts, slings, tremendous pain, and hours and hours of therapy to endure, but one of the hardest things was losing the function of his dominant hand. Chloe took it upon herself to help Pa with his therapy and "taught" him how to write

with his left hand. She took her job very seriously and was so patient and loving with him. The idea of love here is that sometimes you can let your grandchild join you in **your** struggles. Chloe witnessed patience, determination and strength in her Pa as she walked that journey with him. Jack's take on the whole thing was to simply add the humor. One day he was so sad and then exclaimed, "Pa is only going to be able to count to eight now!"

- Every time a new grandchild is born I wonder how I can possibly love this one as much as the others and as soon as I see that baby's face, the floodgates open. It is part of why I believe in God so deeply. This miracle, this precious little person, has taken hold of my heart in a matter of minutes! Sweet little Jovita, our newest grandchild, consumed my heart as she drew her first breath.

- Write those first impressions down in the form of a letter or poem and then write a letter every year on their birthday. The box of letters can be given to the child when they are older. I never got it together for the first three grandchildren but maybe I will have it together for my sweet little Jovita!

Leaving Imprints

I originally titled this chapter Legacy but after looking up the definition I realized that wasn't the word I wanted. I continued looking through the dictionary and thesaurus and landed on the word "imprint."

When imprint is used as a noun it means *any impression or impressed effect.* When used as a verb it means to *impress (a quality, character, distinguishing mark, etc.).* I want to show my children quality, character, and definitely leave a distinguishing mark!

The imprint Grandma Stone left on my life was one of deep unconditional love. I always knew she loved me without expectation. I knew she was faithful to read her Bible and pray. She didn't spend time with God because she *had* to but because she *wanted* to.

As it says in Hebrews 13:7,

Remember those who led you,
who spoke the word of God to you;
and considering the result of their conduct,
imitate their faith.
(NASB)

I have always wanted to imitate Grandma's faith. She led me, spoke the word of God to me, and because of her conduct, I wanted to imitate her faith!

I asked my grandchildren what comes to mind when they think of me. My grandson said, *spoils people, nice, white hair, wears black a lot (black is my friend!), funny, fun, beautiful.* My granddaughter said, *happy, fun, crafts, biographies (she knows I like to read them), fairies, and garden shops.* As far as the younger two grandchildren are concerned, we are just starting to work on imprints and I can hardly wait!

I am glad my grandchildren recall funny moments and times when I worried too much. It is all part of being human. But when my grandchildren think of me, I want the first thing to come to mind for them to be love. I want them to feel showered by it, accepted by it, empowered by it, and hopeful from it. Hopefully they will be overwhelmed by my love and soon realize that as deep as it was, it was only a glimpse of how much God loves them.

Followed by this great love, I want them to remember the depths of my faith. May they know from the stories shared with them that life wasn't always easy, but God was by my side every step of the way. May they know that sometimes I struggled with my faith but I always held on and even when I couldn't see God, I believed in Him. May the beauty they see in me not be measured by the amount of gray hair I have, the number of age spots, or the amount of chub on my hips, but by the joy of knowing God that stayed on my face and resided in my countenance.

Questions for the Grandmother

- Look at a picture of your grandmother. What are the feelings you have? What memories flood your mind? What is your impression of her?
- What do you want your grandchildren to feel when they look at a picture of you after you are gone?
- What funny stories will they remember about you?
- What songs will remind them of you?
- What books will they remember reading with you?
- What memories will come back to them to make them feel like they were your favorite (they should each think they were your favorite)?

Making Memories with Imprints

- Get out one of your high school yearbooks and share it with your grandchildren. Tell them what you were like in high school, the activities you participated in, the clubs you belonged to, and the friends you had. Share a story about a special teacher. Your grandchildren will enjoy reading what people wrote in your yearbook and the words and phrases that were trendy then.
- Share photo albums of your grandchild's parent. Share funny stories, lessons learned and special moments. Just be sure to be respectful in what you share.
- Make a family tree and share it with your grandchildren. Write what each person's occupation was and see if there is a common trend.
- Tell your grandchildren something they will be given when they are old enough. Be sure to write it down somewhere so you don't forget what you told them.
- Have a special photo session with each child. Be sure to include in the picture things that have been part of your relationship.
- Introduce your grandchildren to your favorite hobbies and let them participate.
- Plan a special weekend trip with your grandchildren. It can be a road trip or one on an airplane. Either way, it will be memorable!
- Do you have a video of your wedding? What a great way to talk about marriage with your grandchildren!
- Share your favorite Bible story or passage with your grandchildren. Share why it is meaningful to you.

A Letter for My Grandchildren

Jack, Chloe, Tolkien and Jovita,

It is difficult to even know where to start. I would never be able to express how deep my love for you is. It is a love that is stronger than I ever imagined.

We have had some amazing times together and I am grateful for every one of them. I always felt torn between working more hours so I could spend more money on you and lavish you with gifts, and keeping my time sacred and available to you as much as possible. I will never regret spending time more than money.

If I could give you something, it would be the same things I wanted to give your mothers. I want you to be happy children who know how to teach yourselves and have a great love for learning. Your mommas are setting such a great example for you. The two of them have four degrees between them and are working hard on two more.

I want you to have great imaginations. May you be able to experience great curiosity, create adventure, and experience tremendous joy.

I want you to be strong and able to take care of yourselves and handle the storms of life. I also want you to be strong enough to be weak and rely on God.

I want you to know you are loved greatly by your parents and siblings, your Meme and Pa, your extended family, but most of all, loved by God. May our deep love for you give just a glimpse of how much you are loved and cherished by God.

And lastly, may the experiences and lessons of life convince you of your need for God and His beloved son, Jesus. Follow in Christ's ways. Look for God and you will surely find Him.

Love,

Meme

When I first became a grandmother, a dear friend said to me,
"You were born to be a grandmother!"
Truly, I cannot think of a better compliment.

Grandma Names

Abuela (Spanish)
Ami
Amma
Ammie
Big Grandma
Birdie
Bruma (Flemish)
Bubbe (Yiddish, He-brew)
Bulla
Busha (Polish)
Cookie
Dod
Foxy
Gaga
Gaggy
Gigi
Gma
Gramq
Gramma
Grammers

Grammie
Gramms
Grand
Grandmommy
Grandmother
Honey
Little Grandma
Lola (Filipino)
Lolli
Lolly
Mambo
Marmie
Maw Maw
Meema
Memere
Meme
Mimi
Mims
Minnie
Mom mom
Momo

Mom
Moms
Nai Nai (Chinese
Nana
Nani
Nanny
Naunie
Neena
Nomna (Italian)
Oma (German)
Ouma
Sweetie
Tootsie
Yamma (Icelandic)
Yaya (Greek)

Acknowledgments

A special thanks to those who join me in my dreams:

Bill, my husband, encourager, supporter, and best friend, who is always on the road with me.

Bethany and Sarah, my precious daughters who have evolved into my favorite girlfriends. They have listened, helped me dream, and given me four precious people I adore.

Jack, Chloe, Tolkien and Jovita, my loves, my joy, my purpose for writing this book.

Grandma Stone, my inspiration and mentor.

My mom, who always believes in me.

Diane Krause, who, in the literary world, completes me, and as a believer adds grace to my journey.

Lindsey Cousins, who adds beauty to my stories.

Madison Wright, whose artistic talent makes me smile.

Brenda Barnes, who captured my heart by coming up with the title.

Stacey Jeannett, who encourages, supports, and sharpens me as a writer on a regular basis.

Jesus Christ, who makes it all worthwhile.